Books and Chapbooks by A. Poulin, Jr.

POETRY

The Nameless Garden, 1978

The Widow's Taboo: Poems After the Catawba, 1977

Catawba: Omens, Prayers & Songs, 1977

In Advent, 1972

TRANSLATIONS

The Astonishment of Origins, French Poems by Rainer Maria Rilke, 1982

Poems by Anne Hébert, 1980

The Roses and The Windows, French Poems by Rainer Maria Rilke, 1980

Saltimbanques, French Prose Poems by Rainer Maria Rilke, 1978

Duino Elegies and The Sonnets to Orpheus, Poems by Rainer Maria Rilke, 1977

ANTHOLOGIES

A Ballet for the Ear: Essays, Reviews and Interviews of John Logan, 1982

Contemporary American Poetry, First Edition, 1971; Second Edition, 1975; Third Edition, 1980

The American Folk Scene: Dimensions of the Folksong Revival, Co-Editor with David A. DeTurk, 1967

The Astonishment of Origins

The Astonishment
of Origins

French Sequences by Rainer Maria Rilke

Translated by A. Poulin, Jr.

Graywolf Press / Port Townsend

ACKNOWLEDGMENTS

Grateful acknowledgment is made to *Tar River Poetry* (Peter Makuck, editor), in which the following translations first appeared: "Graves," "The Three Carriers," "Gong," "Memories of Muzot," "Lies I," "Lies II," and "Lies III."

Selections from Rainer Maria Rilke's *Duino Elegies and The Sonnets to Orpheus*, translated by A. Poulin, Jr., copyright © 1975, 1976, 1977 by A. Poulin, Jr. are reprinted with the permission of Houghton Mifflin Co.

The original French poems included in this book have been collected in Rainer Maria Rilke *Sämtliche Werke*, Zweiter Band, Gedichte: Zweiter Teil, Insel-Verlag, 1958.

I wish to thank the Research Foundation of the State University of New York for fellowships, the State University of New York, College at Brockport, for a sabbatical, and especially the Corporation and Staff of Yaddo for a residency during which the first drafts of these translations were completed. —A. Poulin, Jr.

ISBN 0-915308-35-5
LC# 82-80422

9 8 7 6 5 4 3 2
FIRST PRINTING

Contents

TENDRES IMPÔTS À LA FRANCE
AFFECTIONATE TAXES TO FRANCE

LES QUATRAINS VALAISANS
THE VALAISIAN QUATRAINS

Preface

This book is the third in a projected series of five
volumes devoted to the French poetry of Rainer Maria Rilke which I have had the privilege to translate
and which is being published for the first time in the
United States by Graywolf Press.

The first volume in the series, *Saltimbanques*
(1978), was a small collection of six French prose
poems by Rilke and issued only in a limited edition.
The second, with a Foreword by W.D. Snodgrass
and issued in a trade edition (as all others also will
be), focused on Rilke's two French sequences, *The
Roses & The Windows* (1980). This volume, *The Astonishment of Origins* includes 14 short sequences,
ranging from two to six poems per sequence, the
15-poem sequence entitled "Affectionate Taxes to
France" and the 39-poem sequence, "The Valaisian
Quatrains." Scheduled for publication in the Fall of
1982, the fourth volume will focus exclusively on
Rilke's 77-poem sequence, *Orchards*, which includes
at least three sub-sequences, "Eros," "Spring" and
"Orchard." And the fifth volume (still untitled at
this writing) will include most of Rilke's remaining
individual French poems, except for a miscellany of
occasional verses and "dedications."*

By the end of this project, we hope to have offered

---

*The Roses & The Windows and *Orchards* are Rilke's titles;
Saltimbanques and *The Astonishment of Origins* are the
translator's titles.

the first comprehensive collection of Rilke's French poetry in translation, as well as in the original, to appear in the English-speaking world.

*　　*　　*

That Rilke wrote poems in French is not necessarily important per se; he also happens to have written two poems in Italian. That he wrote such a substantial body of poetry in French, however, is another matter altogether. As W.D. Snodgrass noted in his Foreword to *The Roses & The Windows*, by the end of February, 1922, when in less than two months he completed all of the *Duino Elegies and the Sonnets to Orpheus*, Rilke had written only a handful of poems in French—28 in fact. By the time of his death in December of 1926, in addition to the many other German poems he'd completed after the elegies and sonnets, Rilke also had written nearly 400 poems in French—a staggering average of 100 French poems per year! In other words, in only four years Rilke wrote more poems in a language foreign to him than most poets write in their native tongue in an entire lifetime. Such a large body of work by one of this century's greatest poets surely warrants our serious attention, especially when the more we read them the more we realize the extent to which they are an integral part of Rilke's canon and probably have been misjudged by most critics to date.

To say that Rilke's French poems are not his "major" work is to belabor the obvious; many of the poems in *Das Buch der Bilder* and *Neue Gedichte* aren't his "major" work either. Just as obvious is the fact that some of these poems are more successful than others; such is the fickle nature of art, even in the hands of a genius. However, serious readers will realize that individually and collectively these French poems bear the unmistakable stamp of Rilke's masterful impetus and imagination at the fullness of his maturity. And at the heart of these poems is much the same vision as that found in the *Sonnets* and the *Elegies*: the poetic transformation of the world as a result of intense attentiveness to the things of this world.

*   *   *

The poems in *The Roses & The Windows* are generally marked by a kind of exuberance and fragility, as well as by an intense inventiveness heaping image upon image that's reminiscent of the energy informing the *Sonnets to Orpheus*—but with a greater measure of joyful freedom. Poem XI from "The Roses" is indicative:

> All that spinning on your stem
> to end yourself, round rose,
> doesn't that make you dizzy?
> But drenched by your own impetus,
>
> in your bud you just ignore
> yourself. It's a world that whirls

around so its calm center dares
the round repose of the round rose.

There is hardly any of that kind of joyfully serious "play" in the poems collected here. Nonetheless, there *are* several moments when, for one reason or another, they unmistakably do evoke *The Sonnets to Orpheus*; one example is the technique in poem 17 from "The Valaisian Quatrains":

Before you can count ten
all changes: the wind takes
the brightness from high
stalks of maize

to throw it on all sides;
it flies, it slides
along a precipice
toward a sister brightness

which, already taken up
in this rough game,
in turn moves herself
toward other altitudes.

And, as if caressed,
dazzled by these games
that maybe gave it shape,
the vast surface rests.

The controlled thrust of that poem's inner rhythm and the manner in which it is resolved in the last stanza is very similar to that found in sonnet 23 of the

First Series to Orpheus. Meanwhile, the device of using essentially the same word as a verb and as a noun in the first poem of "Small Notebook" is also the same as that found in sonnet 13 of the Second Series to Orpheus; in fact, Rilke uses the word "winter" in both poems;

> Oh you, small heart that winters
> out these bitter winter days with us. . . .
> ("Small Notebook")

> For among winters there's one so endlessly winter
> that, wintering out, your heart will really last.
> ("Sonnets to Orpheus" II, 13)

And the third stanza of poem 2 of "Graves" reflects the unique Rilkean imaginative energy found throughout the orphic sonnets:

> The avid hornet has to dive
> before it enters the transparent lair
> of leaning flowers; to be their
> dream, we must come rising from below.

However, most of the poems in this collection are more quietly "serious" and sombre than those in *The Roses & The Windows*; and their tone, though muted and lyrical, is closer to that of the *Duino Elegies* than to the *Sonnets to Orpheus*. Clearly, the thematic and linguistic energy in the opening sequence, "But It Is Purer to Die," is very similar to that in the *Elegies*. Such phrases as "Death is altogether/too much our parent" and "Look at a child's index and

thumb—/so gentle a vise/even bread is astonished"
emerge out of the same emotional and imaginative
wellspring that generates and controls much of the
Elegies. The Angel that appears in the second section
of this poem is essentially the same as the Angels that
appear throughout the *Elegies*; "This amorphous
Angel/who, bit by bit, erects himself on the edge/of
our sufferings: bright, fatal and forceful." And what
could be more quintessentially Rilke (of the *Elegies*)
than the concluding lines of this French poem's third
section:

> Springs deny themselves, and flowers,
> bruised by inattentive violences,
> deformed by vague inventors
> who excite them to the bitter end,
> blossom without saying: Everything's afraid
> of you: poor killers of abundances!

Admittedly, not all the French poems here are
quite so serious, nor do all evoke the *Elegies* quite so
directly. Even the three sequences on "Lies," which
are thematically related to Rilke's passionate hatred
of dolls and masks in the elegies and elsewhere, are
much lighter and occasionally edged with a sense of
humor that's certainly not present in the famous pas-
sage on dolls in the Fourth Elegy. But these are not
elegies; they are lyrics, some happier than others,
some more melancholy than others. Moreover, at a
time when we virtually demand that all poems be
"meaningfully serious" (especially when written by
"great poets"), some of these lyrics may strike

readers as being just too slight in subject matter. A poem like "Belltower's Song" (12 from "The Valaisian Quatrains") is a clear case in point:

BELLTOWER'S SONG

More than a common tower,
I warm myself to ripen my carillon.
Let it be sweet, let it be good
to the Valaisian women.

I share my manna with them
every Sunday, tone by tone;
let my carillon be good
to the Valaisian women.

Let it be good, let it be sweet;
in the hamlets on Saturday night,
let my carillon fall in drops on
the Valaisian women's Valaisian men.

That, from Rilke!? And yet, to dismiss this poem as too slight is to ignore and to deprive ourselves of the pleasure of discovering the subtle and delicate sexuality of metaphor at work in this small poem, especially in that unexpected turn in the last stanza.

These French lyrics do not directly undertake great subjects and themes. Rather, they are small poems of careful attentiveness to the things of this world, to the common things of this world, and to the elusive states of being in which the world is poetically transformed. And perhaps the manner in which these poems call the *Elegies* to mind the most is by implementing in a foreign tongue and with a quiet, gentle craft (when they are most successful), Rilke's grander themes announced in his noted exhortations in his Ninth Duino Elegy:

> Maybe we're here only to say: *house,*
> *bridge, well, gate, jug, olive tree, window* —
> at most, *pillar, tower* . . . but to say them, remember,
> oh, to say them in a way that the things themselves
> never dreamed of existing so intensely. . . .

> And these things, whose lives
> are lived in leaving—they understand when you
>   praise them.
> Perishing, they turn to us, the most perishable,
>   for help.
> They want us to change them completely in our
>   invisible hearts,
> oh—forever—into us! Whoever we may finally be!

And the burden, the struggle of the Rilkean hero, who is also the voice of these French poems, is never to forget that charge. For as Rilke says in the first poem of "Memories of Muzot":

> The naive bread, the common tool,
> the intimacy of familiar things—
> who can't leave them for a little
> emptiness where longing grows.

*   *   *

This is not the place for another full-fledged rehearsal of various theories of translation. My primary concern in this project has been to offer poems that are as successful in English as I can render them, while also remaining as faithful as possible to the French originals. At times, for the sake of the English poem, I have diverted from a more literal translation and opted for what seemed to be a more precise temperamental or emotional equivalent of the original phrase or line. And if the English seems quirky, it's because the French seemed quirky too. (I also believe that now and then the poet-translator must rely on the precision of instinctive equivalence.) However, I hope I haven't simply ignored key words on the hubristic premise that Rilke didn't really mean to use them.

Of course, some phrases remain utterly untranslatable. The last line of "The Flower Carrier" (the first poem in the sequence, "The Three Carriers") is a perfect example. The French text, "ô Légère!" explodes into a veritable bouquet of meanings in this poem's context, ranging from light (as in 'not heavy'), fleet, frivolous, slightly improper and fast (as in 'a fast woman'), to suggestions of being quick with one's hands, thus also 'light-fingered.' There simply is no such multifaceted—or, should I say, multi-seeded equivalent in English. I have had to choose another and clearly more limited kind of resonance for the English phrase.

And then there are some poems that, regardless of the translator, just don't work in English—sometimes because they don't work particularly well in the original either—but must be attempted because they are part of a sequence. "To a Friend" (poem 4 from "Affectionate Taxes to France") may be one of those poems. In fact, even shortly before I submitted this manuscript for final publication, I was tempted to offer only a prose transliteration of the original and invite readers to supply versions of their own. What appears here is my resolution of Rilke's multiple use of the French word *exposé* which is simply *de trop* in English.

No doubt the translator's greatest challenge—especially when dealing with this kind of formal French poetry—is to reconstruct the original French music in English, without inordinate inversions that risk casting the English into the syncopated sing-song of a nursery rhyme, especially if one wishes to remain relatively faithful to the original words and meanings. Perhaps the poet-translator is one of the people in the world who most acutely realizes why music is the queen of the arts: the French virtuoso never has to "translate" the Russian composer's sonata into French before performing it! But perhaps soon a more adept poet-translator (who might also be a musician?) will be able to go far beyond my occasional and approximate rhymes, my modified cadences, and reproduce Rilke's original French music far more accurately than I have.

* * *

A few comments on the texts are necessary. To begin with, the arrangement of the sequences in this book is neither Rilke's nor is it in chronological order according to the date of composition. Rather, the arrangement of the sequences here is my own.

The somewhat strange title of the sequence, "Affectionate Taxes to France," no doubt results from the fact that Rilke lived in France for many years but was never a citizen of that country. (Somehow, "tender" or even "overdue" taxes to France didn't reflect the spirit of the original.) Poem 8 (except for the last stanza) as well as poems 10 and 11 in this sequence also appear in Rilke's other French sequence, *Vergers (Orchards)*.

During the last years of his life, Rilke lived in the village of Muzot (pronouced Mu-zótte), which is located in the Swiss canton of Valais in the Rhône Valley. Thus the title of the sequence, "The Valaisian Quatrains." The last three poems in "The Valaisian Quatrains" are not part of Rilke's original sequence; they appear among his many other miscellaneous French poems. However, since Rilke clearly identified them as "Other Valaisian Quatrains," I have included them as part of this sequence in translation.

While I've adhered strictly to the French texts as they appear in what is to date the definitive edition of Rilke's work published by Insel Verlag, I have taken the liberty of eliminating certain parentheses around essentially grammatical words that Rilke either forgot or chose to omit in his original text. I also have corrected one or two very basic spelling errors, as well as attempted to make the punctuation and capitalization throughout the sequences somewhat more consistent.

*   *   *

One lives with projects such as these for so long that after a while one also fails to notice even the most stupid of errors, never mind the more subtle dimensions of language and of poetry. Thus, I am most grateful to my editor, Scott Walker, to Roseanna Warren and to Helen Byers for having read intermediate versions of these translations and made suggestions for their improvement. Many of these translations' felicities are the result of those three good people's generosity. The limitations are entirely mine.

A. Poulin, Jr.
Brockport, N.Y.
January 4, 1982

The Astonishment of Origins

for Archibald MacLeish
on his 90th birthday

. . . *la vie, à nous, se passe en prélude,*
mais parfois le chant qui nous surprend
nous appartient, comme à son instrument.
—*R. M. Rilke*

Suites brèves

Short Sequences

«*Mais il est plus pur de mourir*»

> *Mais il est plus pur de mourir.*
> —*Comtesse de Noailles*

1

Tout cela pourrait changer: jamais plus
ce regard que les choses intimes
aiment. . . . Ce qui arrive, le pourrais-tu
faire? Ce qui tombe par soi-même,
le pourrais-tu jeter? Mon héréditaire
main? Dis! Tu connais la colère,
tu trembles souvent pour être après
d'un calme étrange qui m'inquiète. . . .
Est-ce moi qui t'arrête? Tu sais
caresser. . . . Mais dans la caresse,
ce trop de douceur qui dans l'autre s'enfonce
n'est-ce point du meurtre déjà qui sans cesse
renonce? Il n'y a qu'une vitre qui nous sépare,
à peine, de la rapide méprise soudaine
du pharmacien qui verse l'abîme,
de l'énorme dépense avare
du crime. Elle est par trop
notre parente, la mort. Le flot
de la vie qui s'accélère,
c'est déjà elle: la mort-mère.

Vois l'index de l'enfant et son pouce,
cette tenaille si douce

"But It Is Purer to Die"

—Comtesse de Noailles

1

All that could change: never again
this look that intimate things
love. . . . Whatever happens, could you
cause it? Whatever falls by itself,
could you throw it? My hereditary
hand? Speak! You know anger—
you often tremble, later becoming
a strange calm that worries me. . . .
Is it I who stops you? You know
how to caress. . . . But in the caress,
that excess gentleness that sinks into the other,
isn't there already murder that forever
denies? No more than a window pane
separates us from the sudden rapid scorn
of the chemist pouring the abyss,
of crime's enormous selfish
waste. Death is altogether
too much our parent. The flow
of life that accelerates
is already her: mother-death.

Look at a child's index and thumb—
so gentle a vise,

que même le pain s'en étonne.
Cette main, toute bonne,
a peut-être tué l'oiseau
et frissonne
de son ultime sursaut.
Sa brusque négation de fouine
qui l'empêcherait, qui l'empêche?

Il y a une brèche
dans notre cœur en ruine.

2

N'osez pas les nommer! De Demi-Dieux à peine
à notre bouche obscure sont permis. . . .
Et l'âme même d'insistance pleine
ne connaît que cet Ange indécis
qui peu à peu s'érige sur le bord
de nos souffrances: clair, fatal et fort,
ne défaillant jamais et sans vertige,
mais malgré tout, lui-même, être-lige
d'un inconnu et souverain accord.

Lui, Majuscule, Lettre verticale
du mot que, lentement, nous défaisons;
borne d'airain de notre vie natale,
mesure anonyme de ces monts
qui forment une chaîne dans le cœur

even bread is astonished.
Utterly good, perhaps
that hand has killed a bird
and trembles
with its final spasm.
Its quick, weasel–like denial
that would stop it, who stops it?

There is a gap
in our ruined heart.

2

Do not dare name them! Half–gods
hardly are allowed in our dark mouths. . . .
And, even full of insistence, the soul
knows only this amorphous Angel
who, bit by bit, erects himself on the edge
of our sufferings: bright, fatal and forceful,
never flinching, never afraid of heights,
but for all that, himself the vassal–being
of an unknown and sovereign contract.

Him, Capital, vertical Letter
of the word that, slowly, we demolish;
brass boundary of our native life,
anonymous measure of those mountains
forming a chain in our heart,

en sa partie abrupte et sauvage. . . .
Statue du port, phare de l'abordage,
et, pourtant, des naufrages contempteur!

Vivre par lui, c'est notre but ultime,
entre l'enfance lente et le crime,
vivre par lui dans un élan si vrai,
que sa rigueur de roche qui se tait
finit par changer de silence . . . pour
taire un consentement. . . .

3

Renoncez, pieux clients! Les cierges allumés
n'ont plus le pouvoir de remuer les ombres
dans ces visages peints et rajustés qu'encombre
l'indifférent vernis de vétusté.
Reconcez doucement à demander l'avis
de ces partants que la prière offusque;
il leur a bien fallu des cœurs plus brusques
pour être de leurs cris ravis.

Renoncez à ce marchandage doux.

Mais en vous-mêmes, tout au fond de vous,
quel cimetière! Que de Dieux absous,
congédiés, oubliés, hors d'usage,
que de prophètes, que de mages

in its abrupt and savage part. . . .
Harbor statue, landing beacon,
and yet, contemptuous shipwrecks!

Between slow childhood and the crime,
our final goal is to live in him,
to live in him in so true an impulse
that, silencing itself, his rock-rigor
ends up being changed by silence . . .
to silence an agreement. . . .

3

Pious clients, give up! Those lighted candles
are no longer powerful enough to move the shadows
on those painted, readjusted faces
burdened by the indifferent varnish of decay.
Softly give up asking the advice
of the departed dazzled by prayer;
they surely needed blunter hearts
to be ravished by their cries.

Give up this sweet haggling.

But inside you, at the very depths of you,
what a cemetery! So many Gods acquitted,
dismissed, forgotten, out of use,
so many prophets, so many wise men

abandonnés par votre désir fou!

Vous avez dépeuplé les cieux immenses.
Et les dryades privées de leur chance,
sont rentrées dans les arbres et n'avancent
que dans la sève, versant pleurs et pleurs. . . .
Les sources se renient, et les fleurs
brisées par de distraites violences,
déformées par de vagues inventeurs
qui les excitent à outrance,
fleurissent sans se dire. . . . Tout a peur
de vous: pauvres tueurs des abondances!

4

Sur la crête du cœur hésitant:
quel sourire qui de la bouche
s'empare de celui qui hésite!
Quelle lenteur inédite
dans ce sourire. Quel chant
supprimé, dans ce sourire. Autant
de sérieux, autant de limite
que d'affranchissement.
Autant de fuite que de retour.
Quel sourire! On le dirait provocant
n'était-il pas, dans sa double audace,
trop complet, trop absent
pour avoir quiconque en face.

abandoned by your mad desire!

You have unpeopled the vast heavens.
And the dryads, deprived of their chance,
have re-entered the trees and advance
only in sap, spilling tears and tears. . . .
Springs deny themselves, and flowers,
bruised by inattentive violences,
deformed by vague inventors
who excite them to the bitter end,
blossom without saying: Everything's afraid
of you: poor killers of abundances.

4

On the crest of the hesitating heart:
what a smile seizes
the mouth of the hesitant!
What unprecedented slowness
in that smile. What suppressed
song in that smile. And as much
gravity, as much limit
as emancipation.
As much flight as return.
What a smile! We'd call it provocative
if, in its double audacity, it weren't
too complete, too absent
to face anyone.

Tombeaux

1

C'est donc à cela que ta vie fut un tendre prélude,
les inavoués, les absents se montrent ton cœur!
Au lieu de t'appeler au soleil à la fin des études,
on évite ton nom comme le nom d'une peur.

On évite ton nom que la pierre proclame sienne,
car l'événement qui aux pierres confère nos noms
pèse sur les voix des êtres qui se souviennent
cherchant de leur main égarée un aveu de leur front.

C'est donc à cela, à cette musique parfaite
que tout en toi consentait, amante et sœur.
La terre te chante; on sent l'élan de sa tête,
mais sa bouche est tournée ailleurs.

2

Encor, encor, je vais et je m'incline
devant la lente vie de ton tombeau,
à la pervenche et à l'aubépine
tu as cédé la paix de ton enclos.

Graves

1

It was to this, then, that your life was a tender prelude:
the unavowed, the absent show themselves your heart!
Instead of calling you to sunlight at the end of etudes,
we avoid your name like the name of some fear.

We avoid your name that stone proclaims its own,
for the event that confers our names on stone
weighs on the voices of those who recall
looking for their brow's consent with frantic hand.

It was to this, then, to this perfect music
that all in you consented, lover and sister.
The earth sings you; we feel the tilt of its head,
but its mouth is turned toward someplace else.

2

Again and again, I go and I lean
before the slow life of your grave;
you have surrendered your enclosure's peace
to the periwinkle and the hawthorn.

Un jeune été a recouvert la dalle.
Tant de verdure vivant entre nous!
Et tu me tends la pâle digitale
où l'on n'accède que par en dessous.

Il faut que le frelon avide plonge
avant d'entrer dans l'antre transparent
des fleurs penchées; pour être de leur songe
on doit venir d'en bas ressurgissant.

Sommes-nous hauts, nous autres, les vivants,
et trop loin de la prochaine pose!
Le lit même nous soulève et l'on n'ose
te ressembler, Amie, en s'endormant. . . .

A young summer has re-covered the marble.
So much living verdure between us!
And you offer me that pale digital
we cannot reach but from below.

The avid hornet has to dive
before it enters the transparent lair
of leaning flowers; to be their
dream, we must come rising from below.

We, the living, we others who still tower
too far from that future pose!
Even beds prop us up, and we don't dare
resemble you, Friend, as we fall asleep. . . .

Les Trois Porteuses

LA PORTEUSE DE FLEURS

À Jean Cassou et à Ida Jankelevitch

Elles ne sont plus à moi, mes mains,
elles sont à ces fleurs que je viens de cueillir;
puissent-elles, ces fleurs, à l'imagination si pure,
inventer un autre être à ces mains
qui ne sont plus miennes. Alors,
obéissante, je me mettrai à côté de lui,
à côté de cet être, curieuse de mes mains anciennes
et je ne le quitterai plus, l'écoutant
de tout mon cœur, avant qu'il ne me dise:
ô Légère.

LA PORTEUSE DE FRUITS

À Madame la mère de Jean Cassou

Voici ce que c'est que l'année.
Si ronds que vous soyez, vous n'êtes pas les têtes:
on vous a pensés là-bas, ô fruits achevés,
les hivers vous ont imaginés, calculés,
dans les racines et sous l'écorce des troncs

The Three Carriers

THE FLOWER CARRIER

My hands are no longer mine,
they belong to the flowers I've just plucked;
can these flowers, with such pure imagination,
invent another being for these hands
that are no longer mine? And then,
obedient, I'll stand at his side,
at that being's side, curious about my former hands,
and I will never leave him, listening
with all my heart, before he can say to me:
O light-fingered one!

THE FRUIT CARRIER

So this is what the year is.
Round as you are, you still are not heads:
you were thought of out there, O ripened fruit,
the winters imagined you, calculated you,
in the roots, under the bark of trunks

(à la lampe).
Mais sans doute êtes-vous plus beaux
que tous ces projets, ô vous, les œuvres aimées.
Et moi, je vous porte. Votre poids
me rend plus sérieuse que je ne suis.
J'exprime malgré moi je ne sais quel regret
semblable à celui de la fiancée étonnée
lorsqu'elle s'en va embrasser,
une à une, ses pâles amies d'enfance.

LA PORTEUSE DE L'EAU

À Madame et à Monsieur André Wurmser

Toi, qui semblais toute hâte à la fontaine,
depuis que je t'ai arrêtée dans ma cruche,
eau simple, quel calme t'occupe et que tu me pèses
de tes souvenirs. N'oublie rien! Car il faudra
que, rapidement, tu te racontes
sur la pente de notre soif, ô jeunesse liquide!
Ce n'est pas moi qui porterai atteinte
à ta nature en te serrant contre moi. Si tu savais
combien mes lèvres sont fraîches, même avant t'avoir bue;
et si mon cœur soudain me surmonte,
c'est comme le chant du rossignol:
demande-lui s'il connaît la sueur.

(in lamplight).
But still you are more beautiful
than all those plans, O you beloved works.
And I, I carry you. Your weight
makes me more serious than I am.
Despite myself, I betray some vague regret
like that of the astonished bride
as she starts to embrace,
one by one, her pale childhood friends.

THE WATER CARRIER

You, that in the fountain seemed all haste,
since I stopped you in my jug, simple water,
what calm possesses you and how your memories
weigh me down. Forget nothing! You will have
to tell your story rapidly
on the incline of our tongue, O liquid youth!
I am not the one who will injure
your nature as I hold you close to me. If you knew
how cool my lips are, even before drinking you,
and if my heart suddenly soars over me,
it's like the nightingale's song:
ask him if he ever sweats.

Deux Poèmes

1

Aime-moi, qu'il reste à ma bouche
un peu de ce sourire qui te plaît;
mon bras, trop enfantin, quand tu le touches,
demain, il s'éveillera parfait.

Je ne suis point de celles qui arrêtent
le doux passant, le pèlerin aimé;
il me suffit qu'à jamais je reflète
le Dieu pressé qui m'a comblée.

Mais qu'il se verse, que mon corps d'albâtre
soit le vase à le contenir—
ou bien qu'il me comtemple comme le pâtre
contemple l'astre qui devait surgir.

Two Poems

1

Love me, let a little of this smile
that pleases you linger on my mouth;
tomorrow, when you touch it,
my too-childish arm will awaken perfect.

I am not one of those who stops
the tender walker, the cherished pilgrim;
it is enough for me forever to reflect
the hurried God who has fulfilled me.

But should he overflow, let my alabaster
body be the vase to hold him—
or let him contemplate me as the shepherd
contemplates the star about to rise.

2

Qu'il me soit caché par votre main
ce lendemain trop proche que j'ignore;
ce sera un jour tout autre; son aurore
m'aveuglerait de son essor soudain.

Une fois seule, on sera bien forte
à l'ombre de ce sombre abandon,
mais si vous m'attirez vers sa maison,
faites de façon à me masquer la porte.

2

Let that too-near tomorrow I ignore
be hidden from me by your hand;
that will be a different day; its dawn
will blind me with its sudden soar.

Only once will we be very strong
in this dark abandon's shade;
but if you draw me toward its house,
do so as to camouflage the door.

Gong

pour Suzanne B.

1

Bourdonnement épars, silence perverti,
tout ce qui fut autour, en mille bruits se change,
nous quitte et revient: rapprochement étrange
de la marée de l'infini.

Il faut fermer les yeux et renoncer à la bouche,
rester muet, aveugle, ébloui:
l'espace tout ébranlé, qui nous touche
ne veut de notre être que l'ouïe.

Que suffirait? L'oreille peu profonde
déborde vite—et ne penche-t-on
contre la sienne, pleine de tous les sons
la vaste conque de l'oreille du monde?

Gong

1

A scattered humming, perverted silence,
all that was around changes to a thousand noises,
leaves us and returns: the strange harmony
of infinity's tide.

We must close our eyes, renounce our mouths,
remain mute, blind and dazzled:
with space utterly shaken, what touches us
wants no more from our being than attention.

Who will suffice? The shallow ear
quickly overflows—and, against our own,
do we not tilt, full of every sound,
the vast conch of the world's ear?

2

Comme si l'on était en train
de fondre des Dieux d'airain,
pour y ajouter encor
des Dieux massifs, tout en or,
qui en bourdonnant se défont.
Et de tous ces Dieux qui s'en vont
en de flambants métaux,
s'élèvent d'ultimes sons
royaux!

2

As if we were
melting down bronze gods
to add to them more
massive gods of gold
that shatter as they hum.
And from all those gods
departing in the flaming metals
rise ultimate and royal
sounds!

Das Kleine Weinjahr

1

Le souvenir de la neige
d'un jour à l'autre s'efface;
la terre blonde et beige
réapparaît à sa place.

Une bêche alerte
déjà (écoute!) opère;
on se rappelle que verte
est la couleur qu'on préfère.

Sur les coteaux on aligne
tantôt un tendre treillage;
donnez la main à la vigne
qui vous connaît et s'engage.

2

Comme aux Saintes-Maries, là-bas,
dans l'indescriptible tourmente,
celui qui d'un coup se vante
d'être guéri, s'en va,

Das Kleine Weinjahr

1

The memory of snow
is erased from day to day;
instead, the blonde
and beige earth reappears.

A spade, alert,
already (listen!) works;
you remember green
is the color you prefer.

Then on the hillsides you align
the tender trellises;
you give a hand to the vine
who knows you and agrees.

2

As at the Saintes-Maries out there,
in unutterable torment,
someone who, suddenly boasting
he is cured, walks off,

jetant sa béquille ardente:
ainsi la vigne, absente
a jeté ses échalas.

Tant de béquilles qui gisent
grises sur la terre grise;
le miracle est donc accompli?
Où est-elle, la Vigne? Elle marche,
elle danse sans doute devant l'arche. . . .

Heureux ceux qui l'auront suivie!

discarding his ardent crutch:
so the absent vine
has thrown off her stakes.

So many crutches crumbling
gray on the gray ground;
is the miracle accomplished, then?
The Vine, where is she? She is walking,
no doubt she is dancing before the arch. . . .

How happy are those who followed her!

Souvenirs de Muzot

(en février 1924)
À Alice Bailly

I

Nous vivons sur un ancien sol d'échange,
où tout se donne, tout se rend—
mais notre cœur souvent échange l'Ange
contre la vanité d'un ciel absent.

Le pain naïf, l'outil de tous les jours,
l'intimité des choses familières,
qui n'est capable de les laisser pour
un peu de vide où l'envie prospère.

Mais même ce vide, si nous le tenons
bien contre nous, s'échauffe et s'anime,
et l'Ange, pour le rendre légitime,
l'entoure doucement d'un violon.

Memories of Muzot

(February 1924)
for Alice Bailly

I

We live on an ancient bartering ground
where all is given, all surrendered—
but our heart often swaps an Angel
for the vanity of an absent sky.

The naive bread, the common tool,
the intimacy of familiar things—
who can't leave them for a little
emptiness where longing grows.

But even that void, if we hold it
close to us, warms up and stirs,
and the Angel, just to make it legal,
surrounds it softly with a violin.

II/1

De loin le printemps à venir
nous souffle un peu de sa chance;
notre longue patience
va–t–elle enfin aboutir

à ce que l'on aime reconnaître,
à ce flottant bonheur
qui nous portera . . . , ou peut-être
en sera–t–on le porteur?

II/2

Bientôt ce sera à la vigne
de se remettre au clair;
j'attends déjà qu'on aligne
les échalas comme des vers.

Quel adorable poème
l'on écrira sur les coteaux!
Et ce sera le soleil même
qui le jugera beau.

II/1

From afar the coming spring
breathes some of its possibility
towards us; will our long
patience finally bloom

in what we love to recognize,
in a floating happiness
that will carry us. . . , or, perhaps,
will we be its carrier?

II/2

Soon it will be up to the vine
to restore itself in light;
I'm already waiting for the props
to be aligned like lines.

What an adorable poem will
be written on the hillsides!
And it will be the sun itself
that will rule it beautiful.

Mais d'abord, rentrons au feu.
Ce vent trompeur, qu'il frôle
les arbres, et s'il console,
que ce soit pour eux.

Rentrons à ceux qui écrivent,
et puis, saluons enfin
la tendre saison portative
qu'Alice Bailly peint!

But first, let's go back to the fire.
Let this deceptive wind breeze
the trees, and if it comforts,
let that be for them.

Let's go in to those who write,
and celebrate at last
the tender portable season
that Alice Bailly paints.

Le Noyer

À Madame Jeanne de
Sépibus-de Preux

I

Arbre qui, de sa place,
fièrement arrondit
tout autour cet espace
de l'été accompli,

arbre dont le volume
rond et abondant
prouve et résume
ce que l'on attend longtemps:

j'ai pourtant vu rougir
tes feuilles en devenant vertes:
de cette pudeur offerte
ta magnificence, certes,
les veut à présent punir.

II

Arbre, toujours au milieu
de tout ce qui l'entoure—
arbre qui savoure
la voûte entière des cieux,

Walnut Tree

I

Tree that from its place
proudly rounds out
all around this space
of the completed summer,

tree whose very volume,
round and abundant,
proves and then resumes
what we attend so long:

and yet I saw your leaves
redden while becoming green:
with this proffered blush,
in fact, your magnificence
now wants to punish them.

II

Tree, ever at the center
of whatever it surrounds—
tree that savors
the entire vault of heaven,

toi, comme aucun autre
tourné vers partout:
on dirait un apôtre
qui ne sait pas d'où

Dieu lui va apparaître. . . .
Or, pour qu'il soit sûr,
il développe en rond son être
et lui tend des bras mûrs.

III

Arbre qui peut-être
pense au dedans:
antique Arbre-maître
parmi les arbres servants!

Arbre qui se domine,
se donnant lentement
la forme qui élimine
les hasards du vent:

plein de forces austères
ton ombre claire nous rend
une feuille qui désaltère
et des fruits persévérants.

Muzot, écrit le 12 juin 1924

you, like nothing else,
turned in all directions:
as if you're an apostle
who doesn't know from whence

God will appear to him. . . .
So, in order to be sure,
he develops himself round,
and tends Him tempered arms.

III

Tree that inside,
perhaps, can think:
ancient Master-tree
among the servant trees!

Tree that rules itself
by assuming, slowly,
form that discards
the hazards of wind:

full of austere powers,
your clear shade offers
us a refreshing leaf
and persevering fruit.

Le Petit Cahier

À Mademoiselle Contat

1: *ROSSIGNOL*

Rossignol. . . , dont le cœur
plus que des autres exulte,
prêtre d'amour, dont le culte
est un culte d'ardeur,

Ô charmant troubadour
de la nuit qui te hante,
tu brodes l'échelle sonnante
sur son abîme de velours.

C'est toi la voix des sèves
qui dans les arbres se tait;
mais à nous, Rossignol, tes élèves,
tu imposes le même secret.

2: *MÉSANGE*

Ô toi, petit cœur, qui hivernes
avec nous au milieu des rigueurs,
tu te poses—tendre lanterne
de vie—sur les arbres en pleurs;

Small Notebook

1: *NIGHTINGALE*

Nightingale. . . , whose heart
exults more than others',
priest of love, whose cult
is the cult of ardor,

O charming troubadour
of the night obsessing you,
you embroider a resounding ladder
on its abyss of velvet.

You are the voice of saps
that in the trees keeps quiet;
but, nightingale, to us, your students,
you keep assigning the same secret.

2: *TITMOUSE*

O you, small heart that winters
out these bitter winter days with us
—tender lantern of life,
you perch on the weeping trees;

je contemple ce feu qui t'allume
à travers ton plumage dru,
et moi, plus caché à la brume
je ne crains de m'éteindre non plus.

A-t-elle peur de demain cette neige?
En effet, elle durcit en vain;
mais nous, qu'une flamme protège,
nous aurons la joie de demain.

I reflect on the fire shining
through your thick-set feathers,
and I, more hidden by the mist,
I'm not afraid to burn out, either.

Does this snow fear tomorrow?
In fact, it hardens in vain;
but we, protected by a flame,
we'll know the pleasure of tomorrow.

Chanson orpheline

I

Où veux-tu que je m'en aille?
Partout m'attendent ces mots. . . .
Après tous les jours de travail,
après tous les nuits de repos,
après toutes les larmes et les rires
qui se sont écoulées,
après tout que je hais, que j'admire
dans cette chaîne de change
revient le refrain étrange,
qui me fait désespérer.

Est-ce toi mon père? Tu te vantes
que toutes les femmes charmantes
le long de ta vie t'aimaient trop.
Est-ce ma mère, qui chante
dans son pauvre tombeau?

Orphan Song

I

Where do you want me to go?
Those words wait for me everywhere. . . .
After all the days of work,
after all the nights of rest,
after all the laughs and tears
that have slipped away,
after all I hate, all I admire
in this chain of change,
comes the strange refrain
that drives me to despair.

Is it you, my father? You boast
that all those charming women
in your life loved you too much.
Is this my mother, singing
in her wretched grave?

II

Aucune de mes amies
ne m'a compris
quand je pleure dans l'église
elles me disent:
C'est la vie.

Aucun de mes jours
ne me prend par la main,
j'attends en vain,
que je crains:
l'amour.

Aucune de mes nuits
ne m'apporte quelque chose:
une tendresse,
qui me presse,
un rêve, une rose. . . .
Je n'ose
de croire que c'est la vie. . . .

II

None of my friends
has understood me;
when I weep in church
they tell me:
That's life.

None of my days
holds my hand;
I wait in vain
for what I dread:
love.

None of my nights
brings me something:
a tenderness
that holds me close,
a dream, a rose. . . .
I don't dare
believe that's life.

Mensonges I

1

Mensonge, arme d'adolescent,
arrachée à la forge du hasard
toute brûlante. . . . Poignard,
saisi n'importe comment.
Clôture bâclée, brusque mur!
Corps et geste sans tête
auxquels, éperdument, on prête
un visage trop pur.
Plante soudaine et hybride
qui, poussant dans le vide
atteint parfois trois mètres de haut,
et se fane trop tôt
pour n'avoir connu aucune saison.
Maison, belle maison,
trop belle pour nous qui vivons dehors,
maison qui a tort
parce qu'on ignore. . . .
Maison trop durable encore
en face de la mort.

Lies I

1

Lie, adolescent weapon,
torn from the fiery forge
of risk. . . . Dagger
grabbed any which way.
Makeshift fence, improvised wall!
Headless body and gesture
to which, frantically, we lend
a too-pure face.
Sudden, hybrid plant
which, growing in the void,
sometimes reaches three yards high
and withers far too soon
for having known no season.
House, handsome house,
too handsome for us who live outdoors,
house that's wrong
because we ignore. . . .
House still too durable
when face-to-face with death.

2

Toi, ô pauvre, que te cramponnes
et qui, de peur, frémis quand on sonne,
tu as des sœurs si grandes et si pures
que les siècles, à force d'en prendre mesure,
s'épuisent. Adolescent qui se ronge,

ami d'enfance, naïf mensonge,
sens-tu toujours, lorsqu'on te préfère,
dans la révolte qui te redresse,
ta famille pleine de déesses
et ces dieux hautains, tes beaux-frères?

3

Cimetière compromettant,
plein de résurrections évitables;
perroquets ivres de mots palpables
dont leur langue imperméable
s'éprend. . . .
Goût de fruits peints.
Parfum de calices
que de vagues institutrices
avaient brodés sur des coussins.

2

Poor thing, clutching yourself,
trembling with fright when we ring,
your sisters are so grand and pure
that centuries exhaust themselves trying
to measure them. Anxious adolescent,

childhood friend, naive lie,
since you're preferred, in the revolt
that sets you straight do you always feel
your family full of goddesses,
your brothers-in-law, those haughty gods?

3

Compromising cemetery,
full of avoidable resurrections;
parrots drunk on palpable words,
their impervious tongue
infatuated with. . . .
Taste of painted fruit.
Perfume of calyxes
that some vague governess
embroidered on her cushions.

Mensonges II

1

Mensonge, jouet que l'on casse.
Jardin où l'on change de place,
pour mieux se cacher;
où pourtant, parfois, on jette un cri,
pour être trouvé à demi.

Vent, qui chante pour nous,
ombre de nous, qui s'allonge.
Collection de beaux trous
dans notre éponge.

2

Masque? Non. Tu es plus plein,
mensonge, tu as des yeux sonores.
Plutôt vase sans pied, amphore
qui veut qu'on la tient.

Tes anses, sans doute, ont mangé ton pied.
On dirait que celui qui te porte, t'achève,
n'était le mouvement dont il te soulève,
si singulier.

Lies II

1

Lie, plaything we shatter.
Garden where we change place
to hide ourselves better;
or, where we might let out a cry
just to be half-found.

Wind that sings for us,
our own shadow growing long.
Collection of the handsome
holes in our sponge.

2

Mask? No. You're much fuller,
lie, you have resounding eyes.
Rather, a footless vase, amphora
that wants us to hold it up.

No doubt your handles ate your foot.
It seems what carries you, completes
you, is the very movement that lifts
you, so remarkable.

3

Es–tu fleur, es–tu oiseau,
mensonge? Es–tu à peine mot
ou mot et demi? Quel pur silence
t'entoure, bel îlot nouveau
dont les cartes ignorent la provenance.

Tard–venu de la création,
œuvre du huitième jour, posthume.
Puisque c'est nous qui te faisons,
il faut croire que Dieu te consume.

4

T'ai–je appelé? Mais de quel mot, de quel signe
suis–je coupable soudain,
si ton silence me crie, si ta paupière me cligne
d'un accord souterrain?

5

À ce sourire épars
comment trouver un visage?
On voudrait qu'une joue s'engage
à mettre ce fard.

3

Are you flower, are you bird,
lie? Are you barely word
or word and a half? What pure
silence circles you, lovely new island
with origins that maps ignore.

Late-comer to creation,
posthumous work of the eighth day.
Since it's us who make you,
we must believe that God consumes you.

4

Did I call you? But of what word, of what sign
am I suddenly guilty,
if your silence cries to me, if your eyelid winks
at me with an underground agreement?

5

How can we find a face
for that sparse smile?
We wish a cheek agreed
to wear that rouge.

Il y a du mensonge dans l'air,
comme, autrefois, cette marquise
qu'on a brûlée, toute grise
de la vie à l'envers.

6

Je ne m'explique point.
On ferme les yeux, on saute,
c'est chose presque dévote
avec Dieu en moins.

On ouvre les yeux après,
parce qu'un remord nous ronge:
à côté d'un si beau mensonge,
ne semble-t-on contrefait?

There is lying in the air,
just as, before, the awning
that we burned, utterly gray
from living upside down.

6

I don't make myself clear.
We close our eyes, we leap;
with God at least
such an act's almost devout.

Later we open our eyes
because remorse is gnawing us:
next to such a handsome lie,
don't we seem counterfeit?

Mensonges III

1

On dit: j'ai rêvé, et non: j'ai menti.
On se réveille, on fait la refonte,
rentrant avec un peu de honte
dans la chambre anéantie.

L'ascenseur nous remet à l'étage,
dit «de la réalité» et s'en va.
Et on montre aux choses sages
sa figure de mardi gras.

2

Y a-t-il davantage en fait de mensonge?
Cela dépend du chasseur et de la chasse.
Celui qui revient à la surface
est toujours un autre que celui qui plonge.

Lies III

1

We say: I dreamt, and not: I lied.
We awaken, we do some re-arranging,
re-entering, somewhat ashamed,
into the devastated room.

The elevator returns us to our floor,
says, "a little truth," and leaves.
And to those wise things
we bare our mardi gras face.

2

Is there more, in fact, to lies?
That depends on the hunter and the hunt.
The one returning to the surface
is always different from the one who dives.

Quelques Oeufs de Pâques

(pour 1926)

1

C'était un de ces premiers papillons
qui à peine trouvent des fleurs.
Corde avant le violon,
précoce précurseur.

Que le monde lui semblait grand
et surtout peu meublé;
d'appartement en appartement,
tout était à louer.

Mais les maçons n'avaient point fini,
et le vitrier sifflait tout haut.
Le beau monsieur s'en va indécis:
parmi ces ouvriers peu polis
mettre ses bibelots!

2

Toute fleur n'est qu'une mince fontaine
qui tantôt revient de son élan éperdu.
L'arbre aussi redescend en dedans de sa gaine
comme s'il eût rencontré un refus.

A Few Easter Eggs

(for 1926)

1

He was one of those first butterflies
that barely finds a flower.
String before the violin,
a precocious precursor.

How the world seemed large to him
and so sparsely furnished;
from apartment to apartment,
everything was up for rent.

But the masons hadn't finished
and the glass maker whistled loud.
The fine gentleman leaves unsettled:
to place one's bric–a–brac
among such unpolished laborers!

2

Each flower's only a thin fountain
returning quickly from its frantic leap.
The tree also drops back into its sheath,
as if it had encountered a rejection.

Vous seul, pauvre Dieu, jadis, vous prîtes un tel
recul sur la route de la misère humaine,
qu'on dirait que la longue absence de votre bond
                                        dans le ciel

  commence à peine.

3

  Qui sait, si les Anges ne demandaient point:
  Celui, quand la mort l'enserre,
  rejettera-t-il son tombeau loin
  comme un manteau de terre?

  Dans la mort qui nous glace, il eut trop chaud:
  Il y mûrit sa violence. . . .
  Caressons lentement sur l'Agneau
  la laine de son absence.

Poor God, only you, once, took such
a backward fall on the road of human misery,
that the long absence of your leap into heaven
seems barely just begun.

3

Who knows if the angels didn't ask:
When death surrounds him,
will he throw off his grave
like a cloak of earth?

In the death that freezes us, he was too warm:
He ripened its violence. . . .
On the lamb let us slowly stroke
the wool of his absence.

*Tendres Impôts
à la France*

*Affectionate Taxes
to France*

Tendres Impôts à la France

1: *LE DORMEUR*

Laissez-moi dormir, encore. . . . C'est la trêve
pendant de longs combats promise au dormeur;
je guette dans mon cœur la lune qui se lève,
bientôt il ne fera plus si sombre dans mon cœur.

Ô mort provisoire, douceur qui nous achève,
mesure de mes cimes, très juste profondeur,
limbes de tout mon sang, et innocence des sèves,
dans toi, à sa racine, ma peur même n'est pas peur.

Mon doux seigneur Sommeil, ne faites pas que je rêve,
et mêlez en moi mes ris avec mes pleurs;
laissez-moi diffus, pour que l'interne Ève
ne sorte de mon flanc en son hostile ardeur.

2: *PÉGASE*

Cheval ardent et blanc, fier et clair Pégase,
après ta course—ah! que ton arrêt est beau!
Sous toi, cabré soudain, le sol que tu écrases
avale l'étincelle et donne de l'eau!

Affectionate Taxes to France

1: *THE SLEEPER*

Please let me sleep again. . . . During long
battles it's the truce promised to the sleeper;
I watch the moon as it rises in my heart,
soon it won't be so dark at my center.

O provisionary death, sweetness that does us in,
measure of my heights, depth's fine precision,
the innocence of sap, all of my blood's limbs,
in you, at its root, even my fear isn't fear.

My sweet lord, Sleep, don't make me dream,
and mingle in me my laughs with my tears;
leave me diffused so the internal Eve
won't rise from my side in her hostile ardor.

2: *PEGASUS*

Ardent and white horse, bright, proud Pegasus,
after your run—ah, how your stop is beautiful!
Under you, suddenly reared, the ground you crush
swallows the spark and gives back water!

La source qui jaillit sous ton sabot dompteur,
à nous, qui l'attendons, est d'un secours suprême;
sens-tu que sa douceur impose à toi-même?
Car ton cou vigoureux apprend la courbe des fleurs.

3

Qu'est-ce que les Rois Mages
ont-ils pu apporter?
Un petit oiseau dans sa cage,
une énorme Clef

de leur lointain royaume—
et le troisième du baume
que sa mère avait préparé
d'une étrange lavande

de chez eux.
Faut pas médire de si peu,
puisque ça a suffi à l'enfant
pour devenir Dieu.

To us who've waited, the spring gushing under
your taming hoof is a supreme relief;
do you feel its sweetness mastering you?
For your tough neck learns the bow of flowers.

3

What could those Three
Kings really bring?
A tiny bird in a cage,
an enormous key

from a distant empire,
and the third,
some native balm
of mysterious lavender

his mother had concocted.
We mustn't minimize so little,
since it sufficed the child
to become God.

4: À UNE AMIE

Combien cœur de Marie est exposé,
non seulement au soleil et à la rosée:
tous les sept glaives l'ont trouvé.
Combien cœur de Marie est exposé.

Ton cœur pourtant me semble plus à l'abri,
malgré le malheur qui en a tant envie,
il est moins exposé que le cœur de Marie.

Le corps de Marie ne fut point une chose;
ta poitrine sur ton cœur est beaucoup plus close,
et même si ta douleur veut qu'il s'expose:
il n'est jamais plus exposé qu'une rose.

5

Restons à la lampe et parlons peu;
tout ce qu'on peut dire ne vaut pas l'aveu
du silence vécu; c'est comme le creux
d'une main divine.
Elle est vide, certes, la main, cette main;
mais une main ne s'ouvre jamais en vain,
et c'est elle qui nous combine.

4: *TO A FRIEND*

Mary's heart's so unprotected,
not only from the sun and dew:
all seven swords also found it.
Mary's heart's so unprotected.

Your heart seems to me more sheltered,
despite the grief that envies it,
it's less exposed than Mary's heart.

Mary's body wasn't made of flesh;
your heart lies close beneath your breast,
and even if your grief wants it exposed,
it's never unprotected like a rose.

5

Let's stay by the lamp and say little;
all we can say isn't worth the avowal
of silence lived; it's like the pit
of a divine hand.
The hand is empty, surely, this hand;
but a hand never opens in vain,
and we're combined by this one.

Ce n'est pas la nôtre: nous précipitons
les choses lentes. C'est déjà l'action
qu'une main qui se montre. Regardons
la vie qui en elle afflue.
Celui qui bouge n'est pas le plus fort.
Il faut admirer son tacite accord
avant que la force remue.

6: «L'INDIFFÉRENT» (Watteau)

Ô naître ardent et triste,
mais, à la vie convoqué,
être celui qui assiste,
tendre et bien habillé,

à la multiple surprise
qui ne vous engage point,
et, bien mis, à la bien mise
sourire de très loin.

7: PRIÈRE DE LA TROP PEU INDIFFÉRENTE

Aidez les coeurs, si soumis et si tendres—
tout cela blesse!
Qui saurait bien la tendresse défendre
de la tendresse.

It isn't ours: we accelerate
slow things. An opening hand
is already action. Let's look
at the life that flows in it.
The one that moves isn't the strongest.
We must admire its tacit harmony,
before power starts to stir.

6: *"L'INDIFFÉRENT"* (Watteau)

O to be born ardent and sad
but, summoned to this life,
to be the one who, tender and
well-dressed, is present

at the multiple surprise
in which he's not involved
and, well-off, smiles
at a well-off woman from afar.

7: *PRAYER OF ONE NOT INDIFFERENT*
                        ENOUGH

Help the hearts so submissive and soft—
all that wounds!
Who knows how to defend tenderness
against tenderness enough.

Pourtant la lune, clémente déesse,
ne blesse aucune.
Ah, de nos pleurs où elle tombe sans cesse,
sauvez la lune!

8

Reste tranquille, si soudain
l'Ange à ta table se décide;
efface doucement les quelques rides
que fait la nappe sous ton pain.

Tu offriras ta rude nourriture
pour qu'il en goûte à son tour,
et qu'il soulève à sa lèvre pure
un simple verre de tous les jours.

Ingénuement, en ouvrier céleste,
il prête à tout une calme attention;
il mange bien en imitant ton geste,
pour bien bâtir à ta maison.

And yet the moon, that merciful goddess,
wounds no one.
Ah, from our tears where she always falls,
save the moon!

8

Stay still, if the angel
at your table suddenly decides;
gently smoothe those few wrinkles
in the cloth beneath your bread.

Then offer him your own rough food
so he can have his turn to taste,
so he can raise to that pure lip
a simple, common glass.

Ingenious celestial carpenter,
he lends all a calm attention;
he eats well, imitating your gesture,
so he can build well on your house.

9

Il faut croire que tout est bien, si tant
de calme suit à tant d'inquiétude;
la vie, à nous, se passe en prélude,
mais parfois le chant qui nous surprend
nous appartient, comme à son instrument.

Main inconnue. . . .Au moins est-elle heureuse,
lorsqu'elle parvient à rendre mélodieuses
nos cordes?—Ou l'a-t-on forcée
de mêler même aux sons de la berceuse
tous les adieux inavoués?

10

Ce soir mon cœur fait chanter
des anges qui se souviennent. . . .
Une voix, presque mienne,
par trop de silence tentée,

monte et se décide
à ne plus revenir;
tendre et intrépide,
à quoi va-t-elle s'unir?

9

We must believe that all is well
if such calm follows such anxiety;
we live our life in prelude,
but sometimes a surprising song
belongs to us, as to its instrument.

Unknown hand. . . . At least is it happy
when it manages to make our strings
melodious?—Or was it forced
to mingle even with the cradle-song
all those unavowed goodbyes?

10

Tonight my heart makes
angels sing, remembering. . . .
Lured by too much silence,
some voice, barely mine,

rises and decides
never to return;
tender and intrepid,
what will it unite with?

11

Lampe du soir, ma calme confidente,
mon cœur n'est point par toi dévoilé;
on s'y perdrait peut-être; mais sa pente
du côté sud est doucement éclairée.

C'est encore toi, ô lampe d'étudiant,
qui veut que le liseur de temps en temps
s'arrête étonné et se dérange
sur son bouquin, te regardant.

(Et ta simplicité supprime un Ange.)

12

Parfois les amants ou ceux qui écrivent
trouvent des mots qui, bien qu'ils s'effacent,
laissent dans un cœur une place heureuse
à jamais pensive. . . .

Car il en naît sous tout ce qui passe
d'invisibles persévérances;
sans qu'ils creusent aucune trace
quelques-uns restent des pas de la danse.

11

Night light, my calm confidante,
my heart's not bared by you; (we might
lose each other); but the slope
of its South side is softly lit.

It's still you, O student lamp,
who wants the reader, now and then,
to stop and be distracted at his desk
as he stares at you, astounded.

(And your simplicity supplants an Angel.)

12

Sometimes lovers or writers
find words that, though they erase,
in one heart leave a happy place
that's thoughtful forever. . . .

Because an invisible perseverance
is born beneath all that passes;
without stamping the slightest trace,
some of the dance-steps remain.

13

L'aurai-je exprimé, avant de m'en aller,
ce cœur qui, tourmenté, consent à être?
Étonnement sans fin, qui fus mon maître,
jusqu'à la fin t'aurai-je imité?

Mais tout surpasse comme un jour d'été
le tendre geste qui trop tard admire;
dans nos paroles écloses, qui respire
le pur parfum d'identité?

Et cette belle qui s'en va, comment
la ferait-on passer par une image?
Son doux ruban flottant vit davantage
que cette ligne qui s'éprend.

14: *TOMBEAU*

[*dans un parc*]

Dors au fond de l'allée,
tendre enfant, sous la dalle;
on fera le chant de l'été
autour de ton intervalle.

13

Will I have expressed it before I leave,
this heart that, tormented, consents to be?
Endless astonishment that mastered me,
will I have imitated you up to the end?

But, like a summer day, all else pales
the tender gesture that admires too late;
from our words in bloom, who inhales
the pure fragrance of identity?

And that departing woman,
how can she be made into metaphor?
Her soft ribbon flutters, livelier
than this infatuated line.

14: *GRAVE*

[*In a Park*]

At the end of the path,
sleep under stone, sweet child;
we'll sing a summer song
around your interval.

Si une blanche colombe
passait au vol là-haut,
je n'offrirais à ton tombeau
que son ombre qui tombe.

15

De quelle attente, de quel
regret sommes-nous les victimes,
nous qui cherchons des rimes
à l'unique universel?

Nous poursuivons notre tort
en obstinés que nous sommes;
mais entre les torts des hommes
c'est un tort tout en or.

Should one white dove
soar high overhead,
I'd offer your grave
only its shedding shadow.

15

Of what anticipation,
what regret are we the victims,
we who search for rhymes
for this unmatched universal?

Obstinates that we are,
we pursue our mistakes;
but among men's mistakes
is that one golden error.

Les Quatrains Valaisans

The Valaisian Quatrains

Les Quatrains Valaisans

1: *PETITE CASCADE*

Nymphe, se revêtant toujours
de ce qui la dénude,
que ton corps s'exalte pour
l'onde ronde et rude.

Sans repos tu changes d'habit,
même de chevelure;
derrière tant de fuite, ta vie
reste présence pure.

2

Pays, arrêté à mi-chemin
entre la terre et les cieux,
aux voix d'eau et d'airain,
doux et dur, jeune et vieux,

comme une offrande levée
vers d'accueillantes mains:
beau pays achevé
chaud comme le pain!

The Valaisian Quatrains

1: *SMALL FOUNTAIN*

Nymph, forever dressing
with what undresses you,
let your body be excited
for the round rough water.

You change your clothes,
even your hair, without rest;
behind such flight, your life
remains pure presence.

2

Landscape stopped halfway
between the earth and sky,
with voices of bronze and water,
ancient and new, tough and tender,

like an offering lifted
toward accepting hands:
lovely completed land,
warm, like bread!

3

Rose de lumière, un mur qui s'effrite—
mais, sur la pente de la colline,
cette fleur qui, haute, hésite
dans son geste de Proserpine.

Beaucoup d'ombre entre sans doute
dans la sève de cette vigne;
et ce trop de clarté qui trépigne
au-dessus d'elle, trompe la route.

4

Contrée ancienne, aux tours qui insistent
tant que les carillons se souviennent—
aux regards qui, sans être tristes,
tristement montrent leurs ombres anciennes.

Vignes où tant de forces s'épuisent
lorsqu'un soleil terrible les dore. . . .
Et, au loin, ces espaces qui luisent
comme des avenirs qu'on ignore.

3

Rose of light, a crumbling wall—
but, high on the incline
of the hill, that flower hesitates
as if she were Persephone.

No doubt a lot of shade is seeping
into this vine's sap;
and this excess light trampling
above her takes the wrong route.

4

Ancient country with towers insisting
so much that carillons remember—
with features that, without being
sad, sadly show their ancient shadows.

Vines in which so much power is drained
as a terrible sun turns them gold. . . .
And, in the distance, those spaces
glowing like the futures we ignore.

5

Douce courbe le long du lierre,
chemin distrait qu'arrêtent des chèvres;
belle lumière qu'un orfèvre
voudrait entourer d'une pierre.

Peuplier, à sa place juste,
qui oppose sa verticale
à la lente verdure robuste
qui s'étire et qui s'étale.

6

Pays silencieux dont les prophètes se taisent,
    pays qui prépare son vin;
où les collines sentent encore la Genèse
    et ne craignent pas la fin!

Pays, trop fier pour désirer ce qui transforme,
    qui, obéissant à l'été,
semble, autant que le noyer et que l'orme,
    heureux de se répéter.

Pays dont les eaux sont presque les seules nouvelles,
    toutes ces eaux qui se donnent,
mettant partout la clarté de leurs voyelles
    entre tes dures consonnes!

5

Gentle curve along the ivy,
listless road where goats stop;
lovely light that a goldsmith
would bezel in a stone.

Poplar, in its proper place,
with its vertical opposing
the stretching and the sprawling
of a slow robust green.

6

Silent country whose prophets keep quiet,
    landscape preparing its wine;
where the hills are still feeling Genesis
    and do not fear the end!

Country, too proud to yearn for what transforms
    and which, obeying summer,
seems, as much as the walnut and the elm,
    happy to repeat itself.

Country where about the only news is water,
    all this water giving itself,
leaving the light of its vowels everywhere
    between your hard consonants.

7

Vois-tu, là-haut, ces alpages des anges
    entre les sombres sapins?
Presque célestes, à la lumière étrange,
    ils semblent plus que loin.

Mais dans la claire vallée et jusqu'aux crêtes,
    quel trésor aérien!
Tout ce qui flotte dans l'air et qui s'y reflète
    entrera dans ton vin.

8

Ô bonheur de l'été: le carillon tinte
    puisque dimanche est en vue;
et la chaleur qui travaille sent l'absinthe
    autour de la vigne crépue.

Même à la forte torpeur les ondes alertes
    courent le long du chemin.
Dans cette franche contrée, aux forces ouvertes,
    comme le dimanche est certain!

7

Up there, do you see alpine pastures for angels
    among the dark pines?
In that strange light, almost celestial,
    they seem more than far.

But in the bright valley, clear up to the crests,
    what aerial treasure!
Everything that floats in the air and reflects
    will enter your wine.

8

Oh summer's happiness: the carillon chimes
    because Sunday is in sight;
and the working heat can smell absinthe
    around the crinkled vine.

All along the road the brisk waters
    rush, even in this heavy lethargy.
In this free country with its open powers,
    how certain is a Sunday!

9

C'est presque l'invisible qui luit
au-dessus de la pente ailée;
il reste un peu d'une claire nuit
à ce jour en argent mêlée.

Vois, la lumière ne pèse point
sur ces obéissants contours,
et, là-bas, ces hameaux, d'être loin,
quelqu'un les console toujours.

10

Ô ces autels où l'on mettait des fruits
avec un beau rameau de térébinthe
ou de ce pâle olivier—et puis
la fleur qui meurt, écrasée par l'étreinte.

Entrant dans cette vigne, trouverait-on
l'autel naïf, caché par la verdure?
La Vierge même bénirait la mûre
offrande, égrainant son carillon.

9

The invisible almost shines
above the winged slope;
some of the clear night remains
in this day mingled with silver.

See, the light doesn't press down
on those obedient contours;
and out there, those hamlets, someone
always comforts them for being so far.

10

Oh those altars where fruit was placed
with a lovely palm of terebinth
or of this pale olive tree—and
a dying flower, crushed by an embrace.

Entering this vineyard, will we find
a primitive altar hidden by the green?
Even the Virgin, beading her carillon,
would bless that ripened offering.

11

Portons quand même à ce sanctuaire
tout ce qui nous nourrit: le pain, le sel,
ce beau raisin. . . . Et confondons la mère
avec l'immense règne maternel.

Cette chapelle, à travers les âges,
relie d'anciens dieux aux dieux futurs,
et l'ancien noyer, cet arbre-mage,
offre son ombre comme un temple pur.

12: *LE CLOCHER CHANTE*

Mieux qu'une tour profane,
je me chauffe pour mûrir mon carillon.
Qu'il soit doux, qu'il soit bon
aux Valaisannes.

Chaque dimanche, ton par ton,
je leur jette ma manne;
qu'il soit bon, mon carillon,
aux Valaisannes.

Qu'il soit doux, qu'il soit bon;
samedi soir dans les channes
tombe en gouttes mon carillon
aux Valaisans des Valaisannes.

11

Even so, let us bring all that feeds
us to this sanctuary: bread, salt,
this lovely grape . . . and amaze the mother
with the immense maternal kingdom.

Through the ages this chapel
binds ancient gods to future gods,
and this ancient oak, this magnus-tree,
offers its shade like a pure temple.

12: *BELLTOWER'S SONG*

More than a common tower,
I warm myself to ripen my carillon.
Let it be sweet, let it be good
to the Valaisian women.

I share my manna with them
every Sunday, tone by tone;
let my carillon be good
to the Valaisian women.

Let it be good, let it be sweet;
in the hamlets on Saturday night,
let my carillon fall in drops on
the Valaisian women's Valaisian men.

13

L'année tourne autour du pivot
de la constance paysanne;
la Vierge et Sainte Anne
disent chacune leur mot.

D'autres paroles s'ajoutent
plus anciennes encor—
elles bénissent toutes,
et de la terre sort

cette verdure soumise
qui, par un long effort,
donne la grappe prise
entre nous et les morts.

14

Un rose mauve dans les hautes herbes,
un gris soumis, la vigne alignée. . . .
Mais au-dessus des pentes, la superbe
d'un ciel qui reçoit, d'un ciel princier.

Ardent pays qui noblement s'étage
vers ce grand ciel qui noblement comprend
qu'un dur passé à tout jamais s'engage
à être vigoureux et vigilant.

13

The year turns on the pivot
of a peasant perseverance;
the Virgin and Saint Anne
each have a word to say.

Other words are adding
themselves, even more ancient—
all give their blessing,
and from the earth arises

this obedient green
which, with long, hard work,
yields the cluster linked
between us and the dead.

14

In the tall grass, a mauve rose,
a subdued gray, the vineyard in rows. . . .
But above the slopes, the glory
of a receptive sky, a princely sky.

Ardent country nobly rising in tiers
toward a great sky that nobly knows
a hard past forever forces us
to be vigilant and vigorous.

15

Tout ici chante la vie de naguère,
non pas dans un sens qui détruit le demain;
on devine, vaillants, dans leur force première
le ciel et le vent, et la main et le pain.

Ce n'est point un hier qui partout se propage
arrêtant à jamais ces anciens contours:
c'est la terre contente de son image
et qui consent à son premier jour.

16

Quel calme nocturne, quel calme
nous pénètre du ciel.
On dirait qu'il refait dans la palme
de vos mains le dessin essentiel.

La petite cascade chante
pour cacher sa nymphe émue. . . .
On sent la présence absente
que l'espace a bue.

15

Here, all sings the life of yesterday,
but not in a way that destroys tomorrow;
in their hardy primal powers, we sense
the wind and sky, the hand and bread.

It's not a proliferating past,
forever curbing these ancient contours:
it is the earth content with her own image
and consenting to her first day.

16

Such evening calm, such calm
penetrates us from the sky.
It seems to remake the essential
design in your hand's palm.

The little fountain sings
to hide its excited nymph. . . .
We feel the absent presence
that space has been drinking.

17

Avant que vous comptiez dix
tout change: le vent ôte
cette clarté des hautes
tiges de maïs,

pour la jeter ailleurs;
elle vole, elle glisse
le long d'un précipice
vers une clarté-sœur

qui déjà, à son tour,
prise par ce jeu rude,
se déplace pour
d'autres altitudes.

Et comme caressée
la vaste surface reste
éblouie sous ces gestes
qui l'avaient peut-être formée.

17

Before you can count ten,
all changes: wind takes
the brightness from high
stalks of maize

to throw it on all sides;
it flies, it slides
along a precipice
toward a sister brightness

which, already taken up
in this rough game,
in turn moves herself
toward other altitudes.

And, as if caressed,
dazzled by these games
that maybe gave it shape,
the vast surface rests.

18

Chemin qui tourne et joue
le long de la vigne penchée,
tel qu'un ruban que l'on noue
autour d'un chapeau d'été.

Vigne: chapeau sur la tête
qui invente le vin.
Vin: ardente comète
promise pour l'an prochain.

19

Tant de noir sérieux
rend plus âgée la montagne;
c'est bien ce pays très vieux
qui compte Saint Charlemagne

parmi ses saints paternels.
Mais par en haut lui viennent,
à la secrète sienne,
toutes les jeunesses du ciel.

18

Road that turns and plays
along the leaning vineyard,
like a ribbon that we wind
around a summer hat.

Vineyard: hat on the head
that invents the wine.
Wine: blazing comet
promised for next year.

19

So much solemn black
makes the mountain look older;
no wonder this old country numbers
Saint Charlemagne among

its paternal saints.
But all the youth the sky
can give comes from on high
down into its secret self.

20

La petite clématite se jette
en dehors de la haie embrouillée
avec ce liseron blanc qui guette
le moment de se refermer.

Cela forme le long du chemin
des bouquets où des baies rougissent.
Déjà? Est-ce que l'été est plein?
Il prend l'automne pour complice.

21

Après une journée de vent,
dans une paix infinie,
le soir se réconcilie
comme un docile amant.

Tout devient calme, clarté. . . .
Mais à l'horizon s'étage,
éclairé et doré,
un beau bas-relief de nuages.

20

The small clematis tumbles
from the hedge that's tangled
with the morning glory watching
for that time to close again.

All along the road they make
bouquets where berries redden.
Is summer over? Already?
It picks autumn as accomplice.

21

After a day of wind,
the night is at ease
in an infinite peace
like a docile lover.

All turns calm, clear. . . .
But on the horizon, tiered,
glowing and gold,
a lovely bas-relief of clouds.

22

Comme tel qui parle de sa mère
lui ressemble en parlant,
ce pays ardent se désaltère
en se souvenant infiniment.

Tant que les épaules des collines
rentrent sous le geste commençant
de ce pur espace qui les rend
à l'étonnement des origines.

23

Ici la terre est entourée
de ce qui convient à son rôle
d'astre; tendrement humiliée,
elle porte son auréole.

Lorsqu'un regard s'élance: quel vol
par ces distances pures;
il faut la voix du rossignol
pour en prendre mesure.

22

As someone speaking of his mother
will look like her while talking,
this ardent country slakes itself
by forever remembering.

So the shoulders of the hills
shrink beneath a gesture that begins
in this pure space that hauls them back
to the astonishment of origins.

23

Here the earth is surrounded
by whatever suits its role
as star; tenderly humiliated,
it bears its aureole.

When one look is launched: such flight
through these pure distances;
to take its measurements
you need the voice of nightingales.

24

Voici encor de l'heure qui s'argente,
mêlé au doux soir, le pur métal
et qui ajoute à la beauté lente
les lents retours d'un calme musical.

L'ancienne terre se reprend et change:
un astre pur survit à nos travaux.
Les bruits épars, quittant le jour, se rangent
et rentrent tous dans la voix des eaux.

25

Le long du chemin poussiéreux
le vert se rapproche du gris;
mais ce gris, quoique soumis,
contient de l'argent et du bleu.

Plus haut, sur un autre plan,
un saule montre le clair
revers de ses feuilles au vent
devant un noir presque vert.

À côté, un vert tout abstrait,
un pâle vert de vision,
entoure d'un fond d'abandon
la tour que le siècle défait.

24

Once again the hour's turning silver,
mingled with soft evening, the pure metal,
and it couples slow returns of musical
calm with a slower beauty.

The ancient earth recovers, changes:
a pure star survives our labor.
Leaving day, scattered noises re-arrange
themselves and re-enter the voice of waters.

25

The whole length of the dusty road
the green is almost gray;
but this gray, although subdued,
is touched with silver and with blue.

Higher, on another plain,
a willow bares the bright back
of its leaves to the wind
against a black that's almost green.

Nearby, an entirely abstract green,
the pale green of a vision,
with total unrestraint, surrounds
the tower that this century demolishes.

26

Fier abandon de ces tours
qui pourtant se souviennent—
depuis quand jusqu'à toujours—
de leur vie aérienne.

Cet innombrable rapport
avec la clarté pénétrante
rend leur matière plus lente
et leur déclin plus fort.

27

Les tours, les chaumières, les murs,
même ce sol qu'on désigne
au bonheur de la vigne,
ont le caractère dur.

Mais la lumière qui prêche
douceur à cette austérité
fait une surface de pêche
à toutes ces choses comblées.

26

Proud crumbling of these towers
which, nonetheless, remember—
from who knows when to forever—
their towering life.

This constant contact
with the penetrating light
makes their matter slower
and their downfall harder.

27

Towers, walls, thatched huts,
even the earth we measure
off for the vineyard's sake,
have a tough character.

But the light that preaches
tenderness to this austerity
creates a surface like a peach
on all the things it reaps.

28

Pays qui chante en travaillant,
pays heureux qui travaille;
pendant que les eaux continuent leur chant,
la vigne fait maille pour maille.

Pays qui se tait, car le chant des eaux
n'est qu'un excès de silence,
de ce silence entre les mots
qui, en rythmes, avancent.

29

Vent qui prend ce pays comme l'artisan
qui, depuis toujours, connaît sa matière;
en la trouvant, toute chaude, il sait comment faire,
et il s'exalte en travaillant.

Nul n'arrêterait son élan magnifique; nul
ne saurait s'opposer à cette fougueuse audace—
et c'est encor lui qui, prenant un énorme recul,
tend à son œuvre le clair miroir de l'espace.

28

Country singing while working,
happy working country;
while waters continue their song,
the vine grows link by link.

Country that keeps quiet because
the water's song is only an excess
of silence, of this silence between
words that advance in rhythm.

29

Wind that grips this country like a craftsman
who, from the start, has known his material;
finding it hot, he knows what must be done
and grows enthusiastic with his work.

No one could stop this magnificent momentum;
no one could oppose this fiery defiance—
and he is still the one who takes a long step back
to offer his work the bright mirror of space.

30

Au lieu de s'évader,
ce pays consent à lui-même;
ainsi il est doux et extrême,
menacé et sauvé.

Il s'adonne avec ferveur
à ce ciel qui l'inspire;
il excite son vent et attire
par lui la plus neuve primeur

de cette inédite
lumière d'outre-mont:
l'horizon qui hésite
lui arrive par bonds.

31

Chemins qui ne mènent nulle part
entre deux prés,
que l'on dirait avec art
de leur but détournés,

chemins qui souvent n'ont
devant eux rien d'autre en face
que le pur espace
et la saison.

30

Rather than evade itself,
this country accepts itself;
so it's excessive and soft,
menaced and saved.

It gets along fervently
with the inspiring sky;
it excites the wind and thus
attracts the newest freshness

of that primal light
from beyond the mountains:
the hesitating horizon
rushes towards it.

31

Roads leading nowhere
between two meadows,
as if detoured from their
end by design,

roads that often have
nothing ahead to face
but the season
and pure space.

32

Quelle déesse, quel dieu
s'est rendu à l'espace,
pour que nous sentions mieux
la clarté de sa face.

Son être dissous
remplit cette pure
vallée du remous
de sa vaste nature.

Il aime, il dort.
Forts du Sésame,
nous entrons dans son corps
et dormons dans son âme.

33

Ce ciel qu'avaient contemplé
ceux qui le loueront
pendant l'éternité:
bergers et vignerons,

serait-il par leurs yeux
devenu permanent,
ce beau ciel et son vent,
son vent bleu?

32

What goddess, what god
came back to this place
so we could better feel
the brightness of its face.

Its atomized being
fills this pure
valley with the stirring
of its vast nature.

It loves. It sleeps.
We enter its body,
the Caves of Sesame,
and, in its soul, sleep.

33

This sky contemplated
by those who will praise
it throughout eternity:
vine-growers, shepherds,

this beautiful sky,
its wind, its blue wind,
will it be made even more
permanent by their eyes?

Et son calme après,
si profond et si fort,
comme un dieu satisfait
qui s'endort.

34

Mais non seulement le regard
de ceux qui travaillent les champs,
celui des chèvres prend part
à parfaire le lent

aspect de la Noble Contrée.
On la contemple toujours
comme pour y rester ou pour
l'éterniser

dans un si grand souvenir
qu'aucun ange n'osera,
pour augmenter son éclat,
intervenir.

And after, its calm,
so strong, so deep,
like a satisfied god
falling asleep.

34

Not only the gaze of those
who work the fields,
but also that of goats takes
part in perfecting the slow

aspect of this noble country.
We always contemplate it
as if to remain there, or maybe
to eternalize it

in so great a memory
that no angel, to brighten
its lustre, would dare
intervene.

35

Au ciel, plein d'attention,
ici la terre raconte;
son souvenir la surmonte
dans ces nobles monts.

Parfois elle paraît attendrie
qu'on l'écoute si bien—
alors elle montre sa vie
et ne dit plus rien.

36

Beau papillon près du sol,
à l'attentive nature
montrant les enluminures
de son livre de vol.

Un autre se ferme au bord
de la fleur qu'on respire:
ce n'est pas le moment de lire.
Et tant d'autres encor,

35

Here the earth tells her story
to an attentive sky;
among these noble mountains
she is mastered by her memory.

Sometimes she seems touched
that we listen so well—
so she reveals her life
and then says nothing more.

36

A beautiful butterfly near
the earth is displaying
the illuminations of its flying
book to an attentive nature.

Another closes on the border
of the flower that we breathe:
this is not the time to read.
And still so many others,

de menus bleus, s'éparpillent,
flottants et voletants,
comme de bleues brindilles
d'une lettre d'amour au vent,

d'une lettre déchirée
qu'on était en train de faire
pendant que la destinataire
hésitait à l'entrée.

37: *CIEL VALAISAN*

Comment notre cœur lorsqu'il vibre
a-t-il tant besoin
que tout un ciel de loin
lui donne des conseils d'équilibre.

Mais ce ciel depuis toujours
a de nos cris l'habitude;
ami de la terre rude,
il en adoucit le contour.

fragile blues scattered,
floating and fluttering
like the blue fragmenting
of a love letter in the wind,

of a torn-up letter
we had just been writing
while its addressee
hesitated at the door.

37: *VALAISIAN SKY*

Even as it thrills,
how our heart depends
on a whole distant sky
to offer stable counsel.

But this sky has always been
accustomed to our cries;
the friend of this rough earth
whose contours it tempers.

38

Les hannetons ont fini leur ravage.
À ces rameaux déchus octroyés,
ils semblent pleins et innocents et sages
comme s'ils étaient les fils du noyer.

Et l'arbre même ne se plaint qu'à peine,
car dans son vide guérit tant de bleu.
La vie s'attaque à la vie sans haine.
Elle abonde dans les prés heureux

où les grillons s'exaltent cri par cri.
Tout au milieu des jeunes vignes bouge
la tête d'une fille au foulard rouge
comme un point offert à tous ces i.

39

Simple clocher trapu, au geste du semeur
qui jette aux sillons qu'avaient tracés les peines,
sans les compter jamais, les innombrables graines
d'anciennes sonneries, ces carillons du cœur.

38

The locusts have finished their ravage.
To the sacrificed and dessicated boughs,
they seem full and innocent and sage,
as if they were the walnut's sons.

And even the tree barely complains,
for so much blue heals in its spaces.
Life is attacking life without hatred.
It abounds in the happy meadows

where crickets are impassioned, cry by cry.
At the very center of the young vines
the red–scarfed head of a girl moves
like a dot offered to each i.

39

Simple stocky belfry that with a sower's gesture,
and without ever counting them, scatters among furrows
traced with great pains the numberless grains
of ancient ringing bells, these carillons of the heart.

La fleur qui les mûrit dans son calice pieux,
le beau fruit qui enfin les versa dans les cloches,
sombres bahuts d'airain, mis dans ce grenier proche
du ciel . . . : c'était la vie, la vie de tant d'aïeux.

La lente vie de ceux qui, lassés, laissent faire
du fond de leurs tombeaux, ou de ces autres dont
les crânes entassés au flanc des ossuaires
n'osent plus dire: nous dormons. . . .

Les vieux, les petits . . . , ceux dont le départ précoce
avait brisé un clair et jeune consentement,
eux tous on fait la fleur et rempli cette crosse
d'où est tombé le trop d'un été abondant.

Le plus fort, le plus doux de leur essence pieuse
tombe autour de nous; taisons-nous, écoutons!
Le rythme du labeur, la joie vendangeuse,
de tous les espoirs la vie volumineuse
est entrée dans ces sons et survit en ces sons!

Peut-être, ce retour nous cherche-t-il à peine,
doucement nous frôlant s'adresse-t-il à Dieu,
à ces maisons, ces champs, à cette terre pleine
de tant de volonté et cachant tant de feu.

Mais, pourtant, dans nos cœurs, de leur côté champêtre,
recevons ce semis, dociles malgré nous,
et portons humblement, pour plaire aux ancêtres,
ce laborieux adieu qui les fit durs et doux.

The flower that ripened them in its devoted calyx,
the lovely fruit that finally poured them into bells,
dark brass chests stored in this attic
near the sky, was . . . : life, the life of so many yesterdays.

The slow life of those who, exhausted, from the depths
of their graves no longer care, or of those
whose skulls, stacked on the sides of charnel houses,
no longer dare to say: we sleep. . . .

The old, the small . . . , those for whom a premature
departure broke a bright and young consent,
all those made the flower and re-filled this staff
from which fell the excess of an abundant summer.

The strongest, the sweetest of their sacred essence
falls around us; let us be quiet and listen!
The rhythm of labor, the joy of harvest-time,
the voluminous life of all our dreams
has entered its sounds and survives in its sounds!

Perhaps this return hardly searches for us;
brushing us softly, it addresses itself to God,
to these houses, these fields, to this earth full
of so much will, and hiding so much fire.

And yet, docile despite ourselves, let us receive
this sowing in our hearts, in their rustic side,
and, to please our ancestors, let us humbly bear
this arduous adieu that made them tough and gentle.

The Translator

A. Poulin, Jr. was born in 1938 in Lisbon, Maine, and graduated from St. Francis College, Loyola University and the University of Iowa. He is the author of *In Advent: Poems, Catawba: Omens, Prayers & Songs* and *The Slaughter of Pigs*, a cycle of poems in progress. He is also the editor of *Contemporary American Poetry*, an anthology, and his translations of Rainer Maria Rilke's *Duino Elegies and The Sonnets to Orpheus* were highly acclaimed. The founding Editor/Publisher of BOA Editions, Ltd., Mr. Poulin is Professor of English at the State University of New York, College at Brockport, where he resides with the metalsmith, Basilike Poulin, and their daughter, Daphne.